100 DAYS OF WISDOM

To: BODE
THANK YOU
FOR THE SUPPORT!!
-ERIC

Published in the United States by Live Your Dreams Out Loud Publishing
Cover & Interior Design by Dean Lin

ISBN: 978-1-7348974-0-1 (Paperback)

Printed in the United States of America

Second Edition

contact@LYDOLPublishing.com

100 DAYS OF WISDOM

My 100 Quotes to Live a More Inspired Life

ERIC BIGGER

Live Your Dreams Out Loud Publishing

PREFACE

I was told words can be powerful. I learned that you can use the source of words to affect, inspire, and influence someone. It was through reading a plethora of books, articles, and researching information that I discovered how to use words and expressions in speech and writing. My experiences have shown that citing something important serves a purpose in your way of thinking and others alike. In this book, you will read quotes that I have written; they are thoughts and phrases that have shaped my life, and I am convinced that they will help shape yours. If you are reading this right now, I would like to thank you for the opportunity to share with you the words that empowered me to be successful. These thoughts, phrases, and quotes are my gift to you. Please enjoy!

> There is no friend as loyal as a book.
> *Ernest Hemingway*

THE PROPER WAY TO READ THESE DAILY DEVOTIONS

Read one page a day early in the morning, and then read it once again in the evening. Before you go to bed at night, glance at it again. With this process, you will learn the power of repetition, and you will acquire discipline, because most people would want to move forward and get it over with. But remember, great things take time, and in the long run, you will appreciate taking life one day at a time and conquering your task at hand. So, there is no rush. Read each quote properly so you can succeed in life efficiently. Be diligent!

You may begin to read!

1

IF YOU WANT ADVANCES, THEN YOU HAVE TO TAKE CHANCES! DON'T BE AFRAID TO TAKE THAT LEAP OF FAITH AND MAKE IT HAPPEN. NOTHING WORTH HAVING COMES EASY, AND ANYTHING YOU SEEK REQUIRES DEDICATION! STAY COMMITTED TO THE PROCESS AND DO YOUR BEST.

DON'T LET OTHERS DICTATE YOUR MOOD;
BE YOU! STAY AWAY FROM NEGATIVE
ENERGY AND ALLOW POSITIVE VIBES TO
GREET YOU. WHO YOU WERE YESTERDAY
DOESN'T ACCOUNT FOR TODAY, BECAUSE
THAT PERSON IS ALREADY FORGIVEN.
LEARN TO LET GO AND KEEP LIVING!

3

FOCUS YOUR ENERGY ON THE THINGS
YOU CAN CONTROL. SPEND YOUR
TIME IMPROVING YOUR GOOD HABITS.
MEDITATING AND RESTING THE BRAIN
REALLY HELPS. BE CURIOUS AND
NEVER NEGLECT YOURSELF.
STAY GOLD BECAUSE YOU'RE GREAT!

THE TRUTH WILL ALWAYS COME TO
LIGHT. DON'T TAKE YOUR THOUGHTS
FOR GRANTED. SOMEONE YOU DON'T
KNOW LOOKS UP TO YOU. BE GREAT,
BE GRATEFUL, HAVE AN ATTITUDE OF
GRATITUDE AND DO YOUR BEST WITH
WHAT YOU HAVE.

NO ONE CAN FIGHT YOUR FIGHT FOR YOU, BECAUSE NO ONE CAN LIVE FOR YOU. THINK ABOUT WHAT MATTERS. YOU MATTER! SO, WHY BE MEDIOCRE AND CONDONE WHATEVER? TAKE IT UPON YOURSELF TO DO BETTER AND TO LEARN FROM YOUR MISTAKES. WITHOUT STRUGGLE, THERE'S NO GROWTH.

YOU HAVE TO BE BAD AT SOMETHING BEFORE YOU'RE GOOD AT IT. QUITTING IS NOT THE SAME AS FAILING. GO OUT THERE AND DO WHAT YOU DO BEST. FAIL A BUNCH OF TIMES. SHOW THE WORLD WHAT YOU GOT, AND THEN GROW INTO IT! YOU WILL ONLY IMPROVE. I CALL IT BUILDING YOUR FAITH!

THIS LIFE IS YOURS! DON'T IGNORE THE TRUTH BECAUSE IT BRINGS REWARDS. THE ENERGY YOU HAVE IS NEEDED FOR THE JOY YOU DESIRE. THE STRUGGLE IS FOR THE STORY. THE HEART BRINGS THE TRUTH...BE YOU!

YOU HAVE TO TAKE FULL RESPONSIBILITY OF YOUR ACTIONS. REMEMBER, IT'S YOUR LIFE, NOT THEIRS. STOP POINTING THE FINGER. DON'T MAKE YOUR PROBLEMS YOUR PRIORITIES. DON'T LIE TO PEOPLE SO YOU CAN FEEL THE TRUTH. FORGIVE YOURSELF SO YOU CAN MAKE IT THROUGH.

DON'T WORRY ABOUT EXTERNAL
ACKNOWLEDGMENT. FOCUS ON INTERNAL
FULFILLMENT. LEAD WITH YOUR
ACTIONS AND NOT YOUR MOUTH. YOUR
LIFE DEPENDS ON YOUR TRUTH. TAKE
ADVANTAGE OF EVERY DAY AND COUNT
YOUR BLESSINGS.

10

YOU HAVE TO CONSIDER THAT UNEXPECTED THINGS WILL HAPPEN IN LIFE. WHETHER IT IS FINANCES, HEALTH, FAMILY, OR RELATIONSHIPS, PREPARATION IS THE KEY TO ALL THINGS. BE AWARE AND LET NOTHING STOP OR BREAK YOU. STAY POSITIVE; IT'S ALL IN THE MIND.

11

WHEN YOU'RE FULL OF LOVE, NOTHING CAN STOP YOU! WHEN NEGATIVITY SCREAMS LOUD, LET YOUR POSITIVITY SHINE. BE AT PEACE WITH YOURSELF. FIND THE GOOD IN YOUR LIFE. LET NO ONE TAKE YOUR GREATNESS AWAY. HAPPINESS IS KEY, SO CONTINUE TO BELIEVE!

12

WHEN YOU MIND YOUR BUSINESS, YOU PRODUCE MORE BUSINESS. FOCUS ON YOUR LIFE. DON'T MAKE YOUR PROBLEMS YOUR PRIORITIES. EVERY DAY, FIND WHAT YOU CAN DO TO MAKE YOUR SURROUNDINGS BETTER. A POSITIVE LIFE IS BETTER THAN A NEGATIVE ONE. SMILE AND BE HAPPY!

13

STOP SELLING YOURSELF SHORT, YOU HAVE MORE TO GIVE. BE TRUE TO LIFE AND IT WILL BE TRUE TO YOU. YOUR EXISTENCE TO THE WORLD IS A GIFT. OPEN IT UP SO THE UNIVERSE CAN BENEFIT. DON'T STOP WHEN THINGS GET HARD; KEEP GOING BECAUSE YOU HAVE TO. YOU'RE A WINNER, SO ALWAYS THINK LIKE ONE.

14

DON'T TAKE FOR GRANTED THE THINGS YOU LOVE AND ARE PASSIONATE ABOUT. FIND TIME TO MAKE TIME FOR THOSE WHO VALUE YOUR TIME. COMMUNICATE YOUR FEELINGS AND BE OPEN TO LEARNING. NO ONE IS PERFECT, BUT UNDERSTANDING IS KEY! STAY POSITIVE.

15

STOP PLAYING GAMES AND BE STRAIGHTFORWARD WITH YOUR COMMUNICATION. NO VAGUE LANGUAGE; HONESTY IS THE BEST POLICY. IF YOU WANT SOMETHING IN LIFE, YOU WILL FIND A WAY. IF NOT, YOU'LL FIND AN EXCUSE. BE CLEAR AND SPEAK THE TRUTH IN A POSITIVE WAY.

16

YOU CAN LIVE AN ORANGE LIFE, OR YOU CAN LIVE AN APPLE LIFE. YOU CAN PEEL AWAY AT YOUR JOURNEY, OR YOU CAN TAKE A BITE AND HAVE YOUR WAY! THE QUESTION IS, WHAT ARE YOU GOING DO? DON'T TAKE THE EASY WAY BECAUSE YOU DON'T WANT TO ENDURE THE HARD. EVERY CHALLENGE IS WORTH THE REWARD, AND ANYTHING EASY DOESN'T LAST!

17

EVERY MOMENT COUNTS. INVEST YOUR TIME AND EFFORT INTO WHAT MATTERS. OTHERS' OPINIONS OF YOU ARE JUST A CONFESSION OF WHAT THEY THINK; GIVE THEM NO THOUGHT! FOCUS ON WHAT YOU LOVE AND REMEMBER, EVERYONE HAS FLAWS. WORK ON YOURS!

18

DON'T BE AFRAID TO ASK QUESTIONS.
DON'T BE AFRAID TO MAKE MISTAKES,
BECAUSE THAT'S HOW YOU LEARN!
LIFE IS NOW; STOP WAITING FOR
OPPORTUNITY AND CREATE YOUR OWN.
YOUR MIND IS POWERFUL!

19

EVERYBODY WANTS THE BRIGHT LIGHTS, BUT ARE YOU WILLING TO FIGHT, TO SACRIFICE AND TO DO THE UNTHINKABLE? YOU HAVE TO DO THINGS THE RIGHT WAY. LIFE IS ABOUT HARD WORK AND DEDICATION. WHO ARE YOU NOT TO SUCCEED? LOVE YOURSELF AND WORK DILIGENTLY.

20

THE WINNERS OF THE WORLD WERE ONCE LOSERS. WHEN YOU LOSE, YOU LEARN. REAL WINNERS HAVE LOST TO BE WHERE THEY ARE. NEVER BE AFRAID TO LOSE. LEARN FROM DEFEAT. YOU'RE A WINNER; KEEP GOING AND PURSUE YOUR DREAMS.

21

YOU CAN DO ANYTHING TODAY, AS LONG AS YOU PUT YOUR MIND TO IT AND GO OUT AND GET IT! REMEMBER, ANYTHING IS POSSIBLE WHEN YOU BELIEVE IT IS. MAKE THINGS HAPPEN THAT YOU WANT TO HAPPEN IN YOUR LIFE. YOU MUST WORK HARD AT WHAT YOU WANT, SINCE WHAT YOU WANT WON'T COME EASY BECAUSE IT HAS VALUE ATTACHED TO IT.
STAY DRIVEN.

THERE'S A PERSON INSIDE OF YOU WHOM YOU WANT TO BECOME. THERE'S SOMETHING YOU KNOW YOU NEED TO DO. REMEMBER, NO ONE CAN BE YOU MORE THAN YOU! THE KEY IS TO BE HONEST WITH YOURSELF AND TO MAKE A DECISION. DON'T WAIT UNTIL IT'S TOO LATE TO MAKE A COMMITMENT!

23

IF YOU WANT MORE OUT OF LIFE,
YOU HAVE TO DO MORE. RAISE YOUR
STANDARD OF LIVING AND FOCUS
ON PROGRESS. ALWAYS REMEMBER
WHATEVER YOU CAN IMAGINE IS POSSIBLE
BECAUSE YOU HAVE THE MIND TO SEE IT...
NOW BELIEVE IT!

24

LET'S GET THE BALL ROLLING. DON'T COMPLAIN; MAINTAIN. DON'T LAG; MAKE A DIFFERENCE! DON'T WAIT; CREATE! MAKE YOUR NEXT MOVE BETTER THAN YOUR PREVIOUS MOVE TO KEEP MOMENTUM GOING. WHAT'S LIFE WITHOUT SACRIFICE? CHALLENGE YOURSELF!

25

THE GAIN IS IN THE PAIN. LISTEN TO YOUR INTUITION; DON'T BE STUBBORN! IF YOU CAN DO SOMETHING, THEN GET IT DONE. DON'T LIE TO YOURSELF; HONOR YOURSELF. YOU'RE POWERFUL WHEN YOU UNDERSTAND YOURSELF, AND THAT'S A TRUE BLESSING. DON'T TAKE THIS LIFE FOR GRANTED.

SOME PEOPLE WHO LOVE YOU WILL
LIE TO YOU. SOME PEOPLE WHO DON'T
KNOW YOU WILL SUPPORT YOU. YOU
HAVE STRANGERS UNAWARE WHO
BELIEVE IN YOU! BUT YOU MUST BELIEVE
IN YOURSELF. STOP BEING SO HARD ON
YOURSELF. DON'T SETTLE FOR LESS WHEN
YOU'RE WORTH MORE.

LET GO OF THE HURT, LET GO OF THE PAIN, LET GO OF THE UNGRATEFUL PEOPLE IN YOUR LIFE. KEEP GOING, KEEP PUSHING, KEEP IMPROVING. LOVE YOURSELF AND WORK HARD! NEVER GIVE UP. WHEN YOU THINK YOU CAN'T, YOU MUST!

28

WHEN THERE'S SOMETHING WRONG, ADDRESS IT. WHEN YOU'RE FEELING GOOD, SHOW IT! IF LIFE'S SIGNS ARE NOT POSITIVE OR UPLIFTING, DON'T CONDONE THEM. WHEN IN DOUBT, GO WITHOUT. YOU KNOW WHAT'S NECESSARY FOR YOUR FULFILLMENT. NEVER SETTLE FOR LESS WHEN YOU DESERVE MORE!

29

MANY PEOPLE ARE AFRAID OF THE TRUTH
BUT NEVER SHY TO TELL A LIE. LEARN AS
MUCH AS YOU CAN SO YOU CAN CREATE
OPPORTUNITY. KNOW YOUR WORTH SO
YOU CAN GROW INTERNALLY. DON'T
TAKE THE EASY WAY; DON'T ACCEPT
HANDOUTS. YOU KNOW WHAT MAKES YOU
HAPPY! DON'T BE A COPY. BE ORIGINAL.

30

IT'S NOT ABOUT X'S AND O'S! IT'S ABOUT THE WORD YOU, THE PERSON IN THE MIRROR WHO GETS THE JOB DONE. THAT'S WHOSE BEHAVIOR DEPICTS THE OUTCOME. DON'T RUN FROM YOURSELF; WORK ON YOU!

31

IT'S NOT WHAT YOU GET, IT'S WHAT YOU WILL BECOME THAT MAKES YOU HAPPY! RAISE YOUR STANDARDS, TAKE MASSIVE ACTION, AND NEVER DOUBT YOURSELF!!

32

BE DILIGENT IN YOUR APPROACH;
ESTABLISH DISCIPLINE. UNDERSTAND
THAT YOUR FAITH CAN BE AS SMALL AS
A MUSTARD SEED, BUT WHEN YOU
HAVE CONFIDENCE IN YOUR BELIEFS,
YOU WILL REAP THE FRUITS OF YOUR
LABOR. IN ALL YOUR GETTING TODAY,
GET UNDERSTANDING BECAUSE
WISDOM IS FREE!

33

TALENT IS UNIVERSAL, BUT OPPORTUNITY IS NOT. PUT YOURSELF AROUND PEOPLE AND RESOURCES THAT ARE GOING TO BRING YOU MORE. BECOME AWARE AND DON'T BE SMALL-MINDED. LIVE IN THE MOMENT BUT WORK TOWARDS THE FUTURE. WORK SMART BECAUSE IT BRINGS YOU WEALTH!

34

SOME DAYS ARE LONG, AND SOME NIGHTS ARE DARK. BUT IN THOSE MOMENTS, THE REAL YOU WILL COME OUT. NEVER GIVE UP BECAUSE YOU MUST FIGURE IT OUT. DON'T WASTE TIME WAITING WHEN YOU CAN SPEND TIME CREATING. GO OUT AND MAKE IT HAPPEN. WORK HARDER!

35

TAKE YOUR DREAMS SERIOUSLY, AND
NEVER TAKE YOUR LIFE FOR GRANTED.
MANY HAVE SACRIFICED FOR WHERE YOU
ARE TODAY, BUT WHAT ARE YOU DOING
TO MAKE IT WORTH IT? THE SEEDS YOU
PLANT TODAY ARE SOMEONE'S FLOWER
FOR TOMORROW. LIVE TO GIVE, AND
WATCH YOUR BLESSINGS OVERFLOW!

36

DON'T FORGET TO CHECK IN ON YOUR PEOPLE. DON'T FORGET TO LOVE WITH YOUR HEART. REMEMBER THAT STRUGGLE YOU ONCE HAD? SOMEONE ELSE HAS THAT NOW! VULNERABILITY IS A POWERFUL THING BECAUSE IT TELLS THE TRUTH. NEVER EAT ALONE, AND REMEMBER, YOU WILL MAKE IT THROUGH!!

37

WHAT YOU DON'T KNOW, YOU DON'T KNOW; THEREFORE, IT'S UP TO YOU TO KNOW. DON'T BE IN DENIAL ABOUT YOUR WRONGS BECAUSE THAT'S WHERE YOU FIND YOUR TRUTH! THIS IS EASIER SAID THAN DONE, BUT IT'S EASY TO NOT DO WHAT NEEDS TO BE DONE. DON'T CONFUSE YOURSELF; KNOW YOURSELF. DON'T CHEAT YOURSELF; TREAT YOURSELF!

38

EVERY DAY WON'T BE SUNSHINE AND RAINBOWS, BUT EVERY DAY IS NEW AND DIFFERENT. ADJUST TO THE FORECAST AND GIVE YOUR BEST! DON'T COMPLAIN AND LOOK FOR THE BAD. STAY LIFTED AND LOOK FOR THE GOOD. BE GRATEFUL FOR LIFE AND OPPORTUNITY.

39

THE PATIENCE YOU CARRY WILL BE THE
LIFE YOU MARRY. ANYTHING WORTH
HAVING REQUIRES TIME. LEARN TO GRIND
DAY BY DAY AND DON'T
WORRY ABOUT TOMORROW. FOCUS ON
BEING THE BEST YOU AND UTILIZE YOUR
RESOURCES WITH AN OPEN MIND.

40

NO MATTER WHAT THE WORLD AROUND YOU THINKS, YOU HAVE TO FOLLOW YOUR HEART. GIVE ENERGY TO THINGS YOU'RE PASSIONATE ABOUT, AND DO MORE OF WHAT MAKES YOU HAPPY! YOU WERE GIVEN THIS DAY FOR A REASON.

41

LOOK AT EVERYBODY AROUND YOU; ARE THEY ASSETS OR LIABILITIES? CAN YOUR CIRCLE ADD VALUE TO YOUR EXISTENCE? REMEMBER, TOGETHER WE CAN DO WHATEVER, BUT WHAT'S GOOD TO YOU IS NOT ALWAYS GOOD FOR YOU. IT'S NOT THE QUANTITY OF TIME; IT'S THE QUALITY OF TIME, SO BUILD WITH ACTION TAKERS AND TAKE ADVANTAGE OF THE CHEMISTRY. NEVER SETTLE!

WHEN YOU BECOME THE RIGHT PERSON, YOU WILL NOTICE THE DISTANCE OF PEOPLE CLOSE TO YOU. INVEST TIME IN YOU, LIVE LIFE FOR YOU, AND RESPECT THE PROCESS FOR SUCCESS. YOUR CONFIDENCE WILL MAKE YOU ABUNDANT.

NEVER STOP BELIEVING!

43

IF YOU'RE SCARED, YOU SHOULD PRAY.
IF NOT, YOU SHOULD BELIEVE.
IF YOU DON'T BELIEVE, JUST HAVE FAITH!
EVERYTHING IS GREATER LATER.
DON'T FORGET WHO YOU ARE OR WHERE
YOU CAME FROM. NEVER SETTLE.
YOU'RE SUPPOSED TO WIN!

SOMETIMES, YOU HAVE TO DIG DEEP TO GET BACK ON YOUR FEET. WHEN YOU ASK, YOU SHALL RECEIVE. DON'T SPEND ENERGY BEING NEGATIVE OR UPSET. INSTEAD, FOCUS ON THE GOODNESS OF YOUR SOUL BECAUSE YOU'RE LOVED, NO MATTER WHAT. EVERY DAY IS A BLESSING, SO STOP THE STRESSING.
I BELIEVE IN YOU! LOVE WHO YOU ARE, AND KNOW WHO YOU ARE.

DON'T PUT UP A FRONT WHEN YOUR
VULNERABLE SELF WANTS LOVE.
BE AUTHENTIC AND HONOR YOUR TRUE
FEELINGS. DON'T MOVE ON UNTIL YOU
ACKNOWLEDGE WHAT'S HURTING YOU. FIGHT
THE GOOD FIGHT AND KNOW IT'S NEVER
OVER, BECAUSE EVERY DAY IS A VICTORY!

46

IF YOU HAVE SOMETHING ON YOUR CHEST, COMMUNICATE IT! DON'T HOLD HOSTAGE VALUABLE INFORMATION THAT CAN HELP PEOPLE HELP YOU. WE ALL EXPERIENCE DEFEAT, BUT IT DOESN'T LAST FOREVER. LEARN TO OPEN UP AND SPEAK THE TRUTH, BECAUSE YOUR VOICE MATTERS!

LESS IS MORE, SO LET GO OF THE QUANTITY AND DEAL WITH THE QUALITY. DON'T JUST TAKE ACTION; LEARN AS WELL. WHEN YOU FAIL, GET BACK UP AND SUCCEED. IF YOU SAY YOU'RE GOING TO DO SOMETHING, THEN DO IT! YOUR WORD IS EVERYTHING. DON'T SELL DREAMS; CREATE THEM. REMEMBER, YOU'RE AMAZING!

48

IT'S IMPORTANT THAT YOU LIVE YOUR LIFE FOR YOUR HAPPINESS. SHARE YOUR DREAMS AND IDEAS WITH THOSE WHO BELIEVE IN YOU. EVERY DAY IS A TRUE BLESSING! NO MATTER THE CIRCUMSTANCE, YOU WILL ALWAYS HAVE THE OPPORTUNITY TO IMPROVE. STAY TRUE AND CONTINUE TO LIVE, LEARN, AND EARN!

49

LIFE IS ABSOLUTELY BEAUTIFUL, AND ANYTHING ADDED TO IT IS A BLESSING. LOOK AT YOU: YOU'RE BREATHING! YOU HAVE SO MUCH TO BE GRATEFUL FOR. DON'T GET CAUGHT UP IN YOUR PROBLEMS THAT YOU BECOME THE PROBLEM! EVERY DAY COUNTS BECAUSE YOU MATTER, SO STAY FULFILLED.

50

EVERY DAY IS DIFFERENT, BUT THE MIND IS POWERFUL. WHERE DO YOU STAND IN YOUR HEART? DO YOU LIVE WITH REGRETS, OR DO YOU LEARN AND MOVE ON? DON'T BE LIKE HIM OR HER. BE LIKE YOU! NO ONE CAN STOP YOU WHEN YOU'RE FOCUSED, NOT EVEN YOU. GET THE JOB DONE!

51

IF YOU THINK IT'S GOING TO COME EASY, THEN DON'T WASTE YOUR ENERGY TRYING. IF YOU'RE TOO GOOD TO GET YOUR HANDS DIRTY, THEN YOU WILL NEVER BE SUCCESSFUL. JUST BECAUSE SOMETHING STOPS, DOESN'T MEAN YOU SHOULD. STOP WANTING VALIDATION FROM THE WRONG PEOPLE. LIVE FOR YOU AND DO WHAT'S IN YOUR HEART!

DO THINGS RIGHT THE FIRST TIME AND
LISTEN TO THOSE YOU LOOK UP TO.
EVERYONE HAS SOMETHING TO OFFER,
BUT WHAT WILL YOU GIVE TODAY? DON'T
WAIT FOR THE RIGHT TIME BECAUSE TIME
WON'T WAIT ON YOU. BE PROACTIVE.

53

WHEN YOU'RE GOING THROUGH SOMETHING, NEVER PUT THE PAIN ON THE NEXT PERSON. IF ANYTHING, ASK FOR HELP. NEVER BE A BURDEN TO SOMEONE WHO IS A BLESSING IN YOUR LIFE. STOP HAVING EXCUSES FOR THE SAME MISTAKES; YOU MUST CHANGE! NO ONE WANTS TO BE IRRESPONSIBLE OR LAZY BECAUSE IT NEVER PAYS!

DON'T BE AFRAID TO EXPRESS YOUR FEELINGS. LET GO OF HURT AND ANGER AND ACCEPT PEOPLE FOR WHO THEY ARE. LEARN TO UNDERSTAND YOURSELF MORE. DON'T BITE OFF MORE THAN YOU CAN CHEW, AND MAKE HAPPINESS YOUR TRUE NATURE. SEIZE THE DAY!

WHEN IN DOUBT, DO THE RIGHT THING. DON'T GO AGAINST THE GRAIN. REMEMBER THERE'S A WHY TO YOUR EXISTENCE. RAISE YOUR AWARENESS AND ALWAYS BE CURIOUS.

56

THE MOMENT YOU TAKE YOUR EYES
OFF WHAT'S IMPORTANT, YOU LOSE
FOCUS. EVERYBODY HAS SOMETHING TO
SAY, BUT THEY'RE NOT YOU! ANYTHING
THAT'S NEGATIVE IS A NEGATIVE. KEEP
POSITIVITY, FAITH, AND CONFIDENCE UP
FRONT. DO WHAT YOU BELIEVE IN SO YOU
CAN LIVE THE LIFE YOU WANT!

57

BE IN A GIVING SPIRIT. GIVE TO LIVE. THE
MORE YOU GIVE, THE BETTER YOU LIVE!
GIVE YOUR TIME, GIVE YOUR ENERGY, GIVE
YOUR COMMITMENT. IT'S CALLED THE
"LAW OF CIRCULATION." IT DESERVES
YOUR ATTENTION! THEREFORE, YOU WILL
RECEIVE YOUR BLESSINGS!

58

YOUR LIFE IS ABOUT LIVING FREE AND BEING ALL YOU CAN BE. REMEMBER TO ENJOY THE LIFE YOU LIVE AND NOT TO BE SO HARD ON YOURSELF. HAVE SOME BALANCE! STOP THINKING YOU CAN'T DO SOMETHING WHEN YOU KNOW YOU CAN. SMILE AND BREATHE HAPPINESS!

59

WHEN YOU'RE THINKING ABOUT GIVING UP, JUST KNOW THERE'S A CHILD, A PARENT, A KID, AND AN ENTIRE COMMUNITY COUNTING ON YOU. LET THAT BE YOUR MOTIVATION, LET THAT DRIVE YOU! WHEN YOU LIVE FOR SOMETHING OTHER THAN YOURSELF, YOU BECOME MORE. KEEPING PUSHING. DON'T QUIT! LET'S GO!

61

WHEN YOU MAKE A DECISION, THERE ARE
NO FEELINGS INVOLVED BECAUSE YOU'RE
COMMITTED TO TAKING ACTION TO GET
WHAT YOU WANT! WORK ON YOUR WORK!
PROGRESS AND EVOLVE!

61

DON'T BE AFRAID TO BE VULNERABLE,
BECAUSE THAT'S WHEN YOU BECOME
POWERFUL! THERE'S NOTHING TO HIDE
ABOUT BEING YOU. SHOWING YOUR LIFE
RECIPE COMPLETES YOU, AND THAT'S THE
POWER OF VULNERABILITY WITHIN YOU.
I'M VULNERABLE TOO.

YOU MADE IT THIS FAR IN LIFE FOR A REASON. YOU HAVE TO STAY THE COURSE, RUN THAT MARATHON, AND KEEP HITTING THAT BAG; STICK AND MOVE! DON'T WORRY ABOUT THE PAST; WORRY ABOUT THE FUTURE, BECAUSE IT'S PROMISING!

63

IF YOU COULDN'T FAIL IN LIFE, WHO WOULD YOU BE? HOW WOULD YOU FEEL? WHAT WOULD YOU DO? DON'T MAKE YOUR BIGGEST PROBLEM YOUR BIGGEST PRIORITY. FEED YOUR FAITH AND NOT YOUR FEARS. JUST LIVE!

64

IT'S NOT YOUR TALENT THAT WILL GET
YOU ON; IT'S YOUR DRIVE TO SURVIVE AND
THRIVE IN THIS WORLD. BE DRIVEN TO
BECOME A WINNER. PERSEVERE; NEVER
GIVE UP. THE WORLD IS YOURS!

65

YOU HAVE TO BE WILLING TO FAIL
PUBLICLY TO GROW PERSONALLY.
WHETHER YOU FAILED OR SUCCEEDED
IS IRRELEVANT TO WHAT YOU HAVE
LEARNED. DON'T BE AFRAID TO STAND
OUT IN A VULNERABLE STATE. BE GREAT.
LOVE THE TRUTH; IT'S ALL ABOUT YOU!

"

WHEN THE UNEXPECTED HAPPENS
IN YOUR LIFE, REMAIN POSITIVE, AND
REMEMBER THAT REACTING IS A HABIT.
TO RESPOND, YOU HAVE TO THINK!
THINK BEFORE YOU TAKE THE WRONG
ACTIONS. KEEP IT MOVING AND
STAY POSITIVE.

TAKE WHAT YOU LEARNED AND APPLY
WHAT YOU KNOW FOR YOUR GROWTH.
IN ORDER TO BE FREE, YOU HAVE TO BE
YOU! IT'S NOT ABOUT WHAT YOU HAVE;
IT'S MORE ABOUT HOW YOU FEEL. KEEP
YOUR EMOTIONAL BANK ACCOUNT FULL
AND ALWAYS DEPOSIT HAPPINESS!

68

TAKE RESPONSIBILITY FOR ALL YOUR
ACTIONS AND LEARN FROM YOUR
MISTAKES. CONTINUE TO IMPROVE. GIVE
NEGATIVITY NO ENERGY AND BE GREAT!

69

THE MOMENTUM YOU GAIN FROM TAKING
THE FIRST STEP WILL GIVE YOU THE
ENERGY NEEDED TO ACCOMPLISH YOUR
GOAL. YOU HAVE TO BE IN IT TO WIN IT!
THE MORE YOU KNOW, THE MORE YOU
WILL GROW. USE YOUR RESOURCES AND
UTILIZE YOUR WORTH;
DON'T BECOME COMPLACENT.

70

LISTEN TO YOUR INNER SELF. STOP
ASKING PEOPLE FOR THEIR OPINIONS AND
MAKE YOUR OWN DECISIONS. FOLLOW
YOUR OWN COUNCIL AND LEAD THYSELF!
BE FREE, BE YOU, LOVE YOURSELF.

71

YOU ARE WHAT YOU BELIEVE AND THINK ABOUT. IT'S NOT ABOUT GETTING WHAT YOU WANT; IT'S ABOUT BECOMING WHAT YOU DREAM TO BE! STICK TO THE SCRIPT. BE GREAT. HAVE AN AMAZING DAY!

YOU HAVE TO CONCEIVE IT ON THE INSIDE
TO RECEIVE IT ON THE OUTSIDE. YOU HAVE
TO LET GO OF YOUR PAST. CHOOSE TO BE
HAPPY AND LIVE TO GIVE. IF YOU BELIEVE,
THEN ALL THINGS ARE POSSIBLE!

73

IF YOU ALWAYS CONDONE MEDIOCRE BEHAVIOR, YOU WILL ALWAYS GET MEDIOCRE. JUST BECAUSE YOU'VE KNOWN SOMEONE FOR YEARS DOESN'T MAKE THEM YOUR FRIEND. STOP RUNNING WITH SHEEP WHEN YOU KNOW YOU'RE A LION. YOU GET OUT OF LIFE WHAT YOU PUT IN. LEARN TO BE YOUR OWN BEST FRIEND SO YOU CAN WIN.

WHEN THINGS GOT HARD, DID YOU STAY,
OR DID YOU RUN? WHEN PEOPLE DOUBTED
YOU, DID YOU GIVE UP? DON'T BELIEVE IN
THE FEARS; YOU'RE MORE THAN ENOUGH.
YOU'RE POWERFUL, AND NOTHING CAN
STOP YOU. YOU'RE PHENOMENAL! STAY
TRUE TO YOU; STAY TRUE TO YOUR SOUL.

75

WHEN IN DOUBT, GO WITHOUT. YOU DON'T
NEED EVERYTHING YOU WANT. JUST BE
GRATEFUL FOR WHAT YOU HAVE TO GET
WHAT YOU WANT. IF YOU DON'T WORK,
YOU DON'T EAT. IF YOU BECOME LAZY AND
HASTY, YOU WILL MISS YOUR FORTUNE!
SO, STAY ON IT.

YOUR ENERGY IS CONTAGIOUS, SO KEEP IT POSITIVE! REMEMBER, YOU'RE A SUPERSTAR! YOU MUST WORK HARD. YOUR EXISTENCE IS A BLESSING TO THE UNIVERSE! NEVER FORGET WHO YOU ARE AND NEVER LET AN ISSUE TAKE YOUR JOY AWAY. LISTEN TO YOUR SOUL; IT SPEAKS!

WHAT YOU SPEAK, YOU WILL REAP.
AND WHAT YOU DON'T DEFEAT, YOU'RE
DESTINED TO REPEAT! STAY HUMBLE AND
BE AUTHENTIC. BE AN ORIGINAL.
REMEMBER, LIFE IS ALL ABOUT WHAT
YOU DO!

78

MAKE IT YOUR BUSINESS TO BE ABOUT YOUR BUSINESS. DON'T STOP GROWING BECAUSE YOU'RE COMFORTABLE. TAKE ADVANTAGE OF LIFE AND ALL OPPORTUNITIES. UNDERSTAND THAT EVERYONE IS NOT YOUR FRIEND, SO BE AWARE! GIVE THANKS TO THOSE WHO HELPED YOU; STAY HUMBLE!

TOUGH LOVE IS NECESSARY FOR THE
DEVELOPMENT OF YOUR WANTS.
DISCIPLINE IS NEEDED FOR YOU TO
BECOME SUCCESSFUL! ALWAYS LOOK
TO IMPROVE, NO MATTER WHAT. NEVER
FORGET HOW IT FELT TO BE DOWN; NOW
IT'S TIME TO COME UP, SO STAY STRONG.

80

SELF-ACCEPTANCE IS KEY! YOU MUST ACCEPT YOURSELF FIRST BEFORE YOU SEEK THE ACCEPTANCE OF OTHERS. WHAT YOU THINK YOU ARE, YOU ARE! VALUE YOUR WORTH AND DON'T BE IN DENIAL ABOUT YOUR FLAWS. ACCEPT THOSE IMPERFECTIONS AND UNDERSTAND THAT THERE'S A LOT OF POWER IN ACCEPTING YOURSELF FIRST!

81

DON'T TAKE ADVANTAGE OF GOOD INDIVIDUALS. VALUE THEIR PRESENCE. IF YOU EXPECT HONESTY AND RESPECT, YOU MUST GIVE IT IN RETURN. BE TRUE TO YOURSELF, BUT NEVER RUIN A GOOD RELATIONSHIP. GOOD PEOPLE DESERVE THE BEST, JUST LIKE YOU!

YOU CAN'T WANT SOMETHING GREAT
FOR YOUR LIFE IF YOU'RE NOT WILLING
TO CHANGE. BE A RISK TAKER SO THINGS
CAN SHIFT. DON'T FALL IN LOVE WITH
COMFORT, BECAUSE YOU MUST LEAVE
YOUR COMFORT ZONE TO GROW.

83

ACHIEVEMENT CAN BE UNCOMFORTABLE TO CREATE. BUT DOING NOTHING AT ALL IS VERY PAINFUL. LEARN TO FIND POSITIVE IN ALL YOUR NEGATIVES AND GO BEYOND YOUR EXPECTATIONS. BECOME SUCCESSFUL FOR YOU FIRST.

DON'T BE AFRAID, DON'T HESITATE, AND
DON'T HOLD BACK. GET BUSY, MAKE
SOME MISTAKES, AND LEARN SO YOU CAN
GROW! GO GET WHAT'S YOURS; WHAT ARE
YOU LIVING FOR?

85

TREAT PEOPLE HOW YOU WANT TO BE
TREATED. LIVE YOUR LIFE WITH BALANCE.
TAKE NOTHING FOR GRANTED. LEARN TO
RELAX SOMETIMES AND APPRECIATE
YOUR IMPERFECTIONS. LIFE IS WHAT YOU
MAKE IT, SO BE SURE TO ENJOY IT.

86

THE PERSON YOU WANT TO BECOME, YOU
ALREADY ARE; YOU'RE JUST NOT AWARE
OF IT. THE THINGS YOU WANT IN LIFE, YOU
ALREADY HAVE; YOU JUST HAVEN'T PUT
YOURSELF IN A POSITION TO RECEIVE IT.
THE LIFE YOU WANT TO LIVE IS YOURS
FOR THE TAKING; OPEN YOUR HEART AND
BELIEVE IT!

YOU HAVE TO PLANT GOOD SEEDS IN LIFE
NO MATTER WHAT YOU GO THROUGH.
YOUR INTENTIONS WILL EVENTUALLY
COME TO LIGHT. SURROUND YOURSELF
WITH GOOD ENERGY AND GOOD PEOPLE.
MAKE YOUR WORTH ABOUT WHO YOU ARE
AND NOT WHAT OTHERS LABEL YOU.
GIVE YOURSELF THE OPPORTUNITY TO
INSPIRE OTHERS!

88

YOU CAN ATTAIN ANYTHING YOU THINK ABOUT, BUT YOU MUST HAVE ACTION BEHIND YOUR THOUGHTS. AWARENESS WILL BE A TOOL FOR YOUR SURVIVAL IN ALL THINGS, SO TAKE ADVANTAGE OF VALUABLE INFORMATION AND APPLY IT ONCE YOU GET IT.

89

LET THE RESISTANCE YOU ENCOUNTER SERVE AS CONFIRMATION THAT YOU'RE MOVING FORWARD. PROBLEMS SHOULD NOT BE A REASON TO POSTPONE YOUR LIFE. YOU SHOULD PERSEVERE; KEEP GOING, SO YOU CAN GET TO THE END OF YOUR DESTINATION AND TELL YOUR STORY! NO GRIND, NO GLORY.

90

YOU CANNOT LEARN WHAT WORKS UNTIL YOU ACTUALLY DO SOME WORK. STOP SITTING AND START MOVING. MAKE YOUR LIFE ABOUT DAILY PROGRESS AND CONSISTENCY. NEVER LET UP WHEN IT'S HARD BECAUSE THAT'S NOT THE BEST YOU! YOU'RE BETTER THAN GOOD, AND YOU WERE BORN TO BE GREAT!

91

LIFE IS SIMPLE! DO WHAT YOU LOVE,
MAKE TIME FOR FUN AND ESTABLISH
SOME BALANCE. PAY ATTENTION TO
DETAIL AND LISTEN TO THE LISTENING.
YOU WILL BECOME MORE WHEN YOU HAVE
MEANING TO WHAT YOU DO.

TRUST THE PROCESS YOU'RE GOING
THROUGH AND MAKE IT COUNT. IT'S EASY
TO GIVE UP, BUT YOU WEREN'T BUILT TO
QUIT; YOU WERE BORN TO EXCEL. LEARN
TO PRACTICE PATIENCE.

93

LIVE WITH UNCONDITIONAL LOVE! NO
FEARS, NO JUDGEMENT, NO EXPECTATION.
LOVE IS REAL, LOVE IS YOU, LOVE IS ME,
LOVE IS "WE!" PLEASE SPREAD LOVE
UNCONDITIONALLY! LOVE YOUR PEOPLE
FOR WHO THEY ARE AND NOT FOR WHAT
YOU THINK THEY SHOULD BE.

YESTERDAY IS GONE. THE OLD, THE MISTAKES, AND THE BREAK-UPS ARE ALL IN THE PAST. WE DON'T KNOW ABOUT TOMORROW. THE FUTURE ISN'T HERE! RIGHT NOW IS WHAT COUNTS. IF YOU SPELL "NOW" BACKWARDS, YOU'VE ALREADY "WON." FOCUS YOUR ENERGY AND EFFORTS ON TODAY.

95

KILL THE EGO AND PUT THE PRIDE ASIDE. HAVE SOME HUMBLE PIE. IT'S NOT ABOUT YOU, AND IT'S NOT ABOUT ME; IT'S ABOUT WE! TEAMWORK MAKES THE DREAM WORK. LET'S MAKE THINGS POSSIBLE AND BUILD AN EMPIRE.

96

YOUR DETERMINATION IS KEY, BECAUSE WITH DETERMINATION COMES PEACE! WHEN YOU ARE DETERMINED TO ACHIEVE GREATNESS, THERE IS NO FEAR OF FAILURE. YOU KNOW YOU WILL WIN! THEREIN LIES YOUR PEACE! STAY TRUE TO YOURSELF AND STAY DRIVEN!

YOU CAN GET BIG RESULTS FROM SMALL BEGINNINGS. BE WILLING TO DO THE SMALL THINGS OVER AND OVER AGAIN, AND YOU WILL MAKE BIG THINGS HAPPEN. IT'S THE INTANGIBLES THAT MONEY CAN'T BUY! REAL FRIENDS ARE ONES YOU DON'T GO LOOKING FOR BECAUSE THEY ARE ALWAYS BY YOUR SIDE. LIVE FOR UNDERSTANDING AND STAY TRUE TO YOURSELF.

98

THE GIFT IS IN THE HEART, AND THE CURSE IS IN THE PAST. SO, LEARN TO LEAD AND NEVER TURN BACK. WHAT YOU WANT DESERVES YOUR ATTENTION, BUT WHAT YOU NEED SHOULD BE PRIORITY! A SETBACK IS NOT FAILURE; IT'S AN OPPORTUNITY TO GET BETTER. EMBRACE YOUR GROWING PAINS BUT NEVER STOP YOUR GOOD SPIRITS!

99

IF YOU SIT AND COMPLAIN ABOUT WHAT YOU DON'T HAVE, YOU WILL NEVER GET WHAT YOU WANT. DON'T COMPARE YOURSELF TO OTHERS BECAUSE THEY DON'T LIVE THE LIFE YOU BREATHE. RESPECT YOURSELF ENOUGH TO NEVER CONFORM BUT TRANSFORM; LEARN FROM YOUR MISTAKES AND MAKE BETTER DECISIONS. FEAR NOTHING BUT YOUR EFFORTS TO TRY.

100

IT'S THE LITTLE THINGS THAT MAKE UP FOR EVERYTHING. THE HEART IS WHERE LOVE ORIGINATES, AND THE MIND MAKES THE CONNECTION! YOU CAN ONLY LEARN IF YOU'RE WILLING TO UNDERSTAND. NO ONE KNOWS EVERYTHING, BUT IF YOU'RE WILLING TO LEARN FROM MULTIPLE SOURCES, YOU WILL HAVE UNDERSTANDING! TRUST THE PROCESS BECAUSE THE JOURNEY IS NECESSARY.

101

YOU HAVE NOW COMPLETED THIS HUNDRED-DAY JOURNEY WITH ME. I HAVE RESERVED A PAGE IN THE BOOK SO YOU, THE READER, CAN OFFER YOUR WISDOM TO THE WORLD. THANK YOU.

PEACE AND LOVE TO YOU.

Wisdom is supreme; therefore, get wisdom.
Though it cost all you have, get understanding.

Proverbs 4:7

ACKNOWLEDGMENTS

First and foremost, I want to thank God for my existence and for everything I have experienced on this journey. I also would like to give special thanks to my family, friends, and supporters; you have all contributed to the man I am today. To Karen Evans, Eric Bigger Sr., Shelia Evans, Jamal Allen, Brittny Bigger, Erica Bigger, Lacey Evans, Ralph Bolton, Courtney Smith, Randolph Edison, Verna Myers, Famane Brown, Cora Bigger, Albert Bigger, Monique Lampkin-Bigger, Kelly Roy, Johnny Higgins, Jeremy Robinson, Derek Wright, Quincy Ndekwe, Ashley Ferrer, Nick and Jeanean Shavatt, Aisha Pinky Cole, Chris Anokute, George Hughes, Jennifer Marie, Marcel Umphery, Anthony Biggers, Jennifer Marie Graham, Michael & Michelle Collins, Michael Truesdale, Mark Cornell, Melissa Busfield, Yolanda Crawley, Dr. Sylvia Rose, Coley M. Speaks, Marcus Moody, Walter Sanders, Dontae Ridely, Lekeisha Hill, Theresa Sandra Scott, Andre Cooper, Rodney Chestnut, Andy Gitipityapon, and Tommy Turner, Shery Zarnegin, Dante Young, Martin Katz, Miles Cooperman, Maria Mallat, Celeste Rodriguez, Michele Melendez, Michelle Hernandez, Nelvin Ocampo, Brian Johnson, Karin Howard I truly love you all!

Elan Gale is the author name for the testimony

Thanks to the authors, speakers, and teachers (Tony Robbins, Bob Proctor, Les Brown, Brian Tracy, Mary Morrisory, Joel Osteen, T.D. Jakes, Toure Roberts, Darell Corbett), who use words in a profound way to stimulate their audiences; you all have inspired me.

To the City of Baltimore, Howard Community College, Hampton University and all my alumni.

ERIC BIGGER

MODEL | ACTOR | TV PERSONALITY

ABOUT THE AUTHOR

Eric Bigger is the founder and principal owner of Miracle Season INC. He bridges the gap for people by believing in them before they believe in themselves, showing them how to have faith!

Eric is a dynamic speaker, mentor, and creative advisor in the rehabilitation of one's life. Highly motivated, positively inspired, success-driven, and fit for life is what Eric embodies.

There are no excuses, victims, or losers in Eric's movement; there are only winners!! No matter who or what you come in, by the time your training is done, you will be a certified winner, not just in a focused area but in life.

The path leading to Eric's purpose in life was no easy trek. Coming from a broken home and having to deal with the adversity of the Baltimore city streets, Eric knew at an early age that the odds were stacked against him. Being a witness to many of his troubled friends and family members throwing their lives away, Eric decided to take a stand from that point on. He had the vision to make the world a better place by changing people's attitudes and outlooks on life.

After completing his formal education, performing extensive research, and going through many life struggles, Eric was ready to take action, not just in his life but in the lives of others.

In May 2010 he landed exactly where he planned: in a land of opportunity (Los Angeles). It was evident early on that Eric showed leadership and encouraged emotional success. It comes as no surprise that his mission is to lead people to their best potential.

Eric obtained two AA degrees from Howard County Community College and received a bachelor's degree, magna cum laude, from Hampton University. He is also a certified fitness trainer and certified practitioner of Neuro-Linguistic Programming.

Instagram: https://instagram.com/ebiggerspeaks

Facebook: https://www.facebook.com/EBiggerSpeaks/

Eric Bigger
"It's Miracle Season"

CONTACT

contact@LYDOLPublishing.com

FOR MORE CONTENT & INSPIRATION
FOLLOW ERIC:

www.facebook.com/EricBiggerPositivity
www.instagram.com/EricBigger